Ladybird  Readers

Top Dog
is Sick

Series Editor: Sorrel Pitts
Story by Catherine Baker
Illustrated by Chris Jevons

Ladybird Readers Starter Level

Title		Phonics	Sight Words
1	Alphabet Book	A—Z	
2	Is it Nat?	s a t p i n	a is it
3	Nat Sits		an in sit
4	Top Dog and Pompom	m d g o c k	and can I into no
5	Top Dog is Sick		got not
6	The Fun Run	e u r h b f l	at get go has off the to up
7	Gus is Hot!		full his of on put
8	Jazz the Vet	j v w x y z qu	be but had he him she tell was
9	Vick the Vet		did well will
10	Dash and Thud	ch sh th ng	if ran then they with yes
11	Big Bad Bash		big long that this
12	The Big Fish	ai ee oa oo	her look see them
13	The Big Ship		let me my too
14	Martin and Lorna	ar or ur ow oi er	all are for
15	Farmer Carl		cut down good help now
16	The Big Dipper	igh ear air ure	as have like said some went you
17	The Silver Ring		come from so stop we what

First, go through the phonemes on page 4, and do the activity on page 5. Then, read the words in the first half of the book, focusing on pronunciation and blending.

The sight words are introduced in the second half of the book, first on their own and then in full sentences.

At the back of the book, there are activities and assessments practicing phonemes and sight words. These icons indicate the key skills required in each activity:

 Spelling and writing   Speaking   📖 Reading

Top Dog
is Sick

Look at the story

First, look at the words and pictures.
Use the words to practice phonics.

Phonics focus

m d g o c k

Mack

Doc Panda

Top Dog

Gock

Dot Cat

Aa Bb Cc Dd Ee Ff Gg Hh Ii Jj Kk Ll Mn

Activity

1 **Look. Say the names.**
Write the letters.

1  Top ....D..og

2  ....ot Cat

3 ....ock

4  Ma..........

5 D..........c Panda

n Oo Pp Qq Rr Ss Tt Uu Vv Ww Xx Yy Zz

Top Dog

Dot Cat

6

Top Dog

Dot Cat

9

Doc Panda

Dot Cat

Top Dog

Gock

Mack

Top Dog

Top Dog

Dot Cat

Gock

Mack

15

Top Dog is Sick

Read the story

Now read the story in full sentences.
Practice using the sight words.

Sight words

got   not

Top Dog can not dig.
Top Dog is sick.

Top Dog naps.
Top Dog is sick,
and Dot Cat is sad.

Dot Cat got Doc Panda.

23

Gock and Mack
got Top Dog socks.

Top Dog picks a comic.
Top Dog sits.

Top Dog is not sick.
Top Dog can dig.

Activities

2 Say the words. Match. 🗨 📖

Top Dog

sits

socks

comic

28

3 Circle the correct sight words. Say the words.

1  He can (**not**)/ **got** dig.

2  He has **not** / **got** a comic.

3  He is **not** / **got** sick.

4  He has **not** / **got** socks.

Assessment

4 **Look. Write the words.**
Say the words.

1

| M | a | ck |

M   a   ck

2

| D | o | c |

3

| s | i | ck |

4

| s | o | ck | s |

5 **Look. Write the correct words on the lines.** 📖 ✏️

not	got

1 Top Dog can __not__ dig.

2 Dot Cat _____ Doc Panda.

3 Gock _____ Top Dog socks.

4 Top Dog is _____ sick.

Starter

Alphabet Book
Starter 1
978–0–241–39367–3 ☐

Is it Nat?
Starter 2
978–0–241–39368–0 ☐

Nat Sits
Starter 3
978–0–241–39369–7 ☐

Top Dog and Pompom
Starter 4
978–0–241–39370–3 ☐

Top Dog is Sick
Starter 5
978–0–241–39371–0 ☐

The Fun Run
Starter 6
978–0–241–39372–7 ☐

Gus is Hot!
Starter 7
978–0–241–39373–4 ☐

Jazz the Vet
Starter 8
978–0–241–39374–1 ☐

Vick the Vet
Starter 9
978–0–241–39375–8 ☐

Dash and Thud
Starter 10
978–0–241–39376–5 ☐

Big Bad Bash
Starter 11
978–0–241–39377–2 ☐

The Big Fish
Starter 12
978–0–241–39379–6 ☐

The Big Ship
Starter 13
978–0–241–39380–2 ☐

Martin and Lorna
Starter 14
978–0–241–39381–9 ☐

Farmer Carl
Starter 15
978–0–241–39382–6 ☐

The Big Dipper
Starter 16
978–0–241–39383–3 ☐

The Silver Ring
Starter 17
978–0–241–39384–0 ☐

LADYBIRD BOOKS

UK | USA | Canada | Ireland | Australia
India | New Zealand | South Africa

Ladybird Books is part of the Penguin Random House group of companies
whose addresses can be found at global.penguinrandomhouse.com.
www.penguin.co.uk   www.puffin.co.uk   www.ladybird.co.uk

Penguin
Random House
UK

First published 2017. This edition published 2019
001

Copyright © Ladybird Books Ltd, 2017

Printed in China

A CIP catalogue record for this book is available from the British Library

ISBN: 978–0–241–39371–0

All correspondence to:
Ladybird Books
Penguin Random House Children's
80 Strand, London WC2R 0RL